GW01605818

LUTYENS AND THE SEA CAPTAIN

LUTYENS AND THE SEA CAPTAIN

Introduction by Margaret Richardson

Scolar Press · London

First published in 1981 by
SCOLAR PRESS
James Price Publishing Limited
90/91 Great Russell Street
London WC1B 3PY

BRITISH LIBRARY CATALOGUING IN PUBLICATION DATA

Lutyens, *Sir* Edwin

Lutyens and the Sea Captain
1. Lutyens, Sir Edwin 2. Interior decorations – History – 20th Century – Pictorial works
I. Title
747′2′0941 NK1980

ISBN 0-85967-646-3

Designed by Ray Carpenter

Printed in Great Britain by

Sunstreet Press Ltd., Keighley, West Yorkshire

Acknowledgements

I want to thank Mary Lutyens, Mr R. W. Day, Captain Day's son, and the Rev. Herbert Ward, who has generously allowed me to read and quote from his own unpublished memoirs.

Margaret Richardson

RIBA Drawings Collection
British Architectural Library

In March 1919 Sir Edwin Lutyens went to South Africa to act as consultant to proposed designs for Cape Town University. On the return journey, in April, he sailed from Cape Town on the RMS *Briton*, became very friendly with its captain, E. W. S. Day, and spent many happy hours designing a perfect house for a sea-captain's retirement. This little fascimile illustrates the fourteen pages of 'Inventry' of the contents of Captain Day's house, and shows Lutyens's wonderful ability to project his imagination into the life of his client: Vita Sackville-West called him an 'imaginative jester of genius'. These drawings were indeed made to amuse, but they are also perfectly conceived in every detail and embody many of his own ideals of what it was best to have in a house. Several of the ideas he used again and again. Lutyens sent the drawings to Captain Day from London in 1919, and they were acquired by the RIBA in 1979 from Captain Day's son, R. W. Day.

By early 1919 Lutyens was almost at the height of his career. He had built all his great country houses: the 'Surrey' houses, the classical houses, Heathcote and Nashdom, the romantic castles, Lindisfarne, Lambay and Drogo. The Cenotaph, Thiepval war memorial and the Liverpool Cathedral project were yet to come. And in 1918 he was knighted for his work at New Delhi, the great Viceroy's House. From 1912 his work at Delhi formed the main thread of his career and he even had a separate Delhi office in Apple Tree Yard. He had visited India six times by 1919 and was well used to a long voyage by sea.

He embarked for South Africa on the RMS *Balmoral Castle* on 26 February. As his companion on the voyage Lutyens had a young war hero, Herbert Ward (fig. 1), who vividly remembers the trip and has made it a chapter in his unpublished memoirs. Ward, born in 1897, was seventeen when the war broke out but immediately volunteered for the Flying Corps. In 1915 his plane was shot down and he was taken prisoner. But later he managed to escape with a

1 Herbert Ward in his Austro-Daimler, 1918. (Herbert Ward)

friend by climbing off a train in broad daylight and walking quite straightforwardly into Switzerland. Their story was not believed at first, but later they were recognised as being the first officers of the war to escape. In 1919 William Nicholson, a family friend and Lutyens's neighbour in Apple Tree Yard, suggested to the architect that he take the young man to South Africa. Ward did have architectural leanings and, if Lutyens agreed, it would be a way of getting out of the services. Lutyens was only too happy to take him.

The *Balmoral Castle* had been commandeered as a transport ship and was full of demobilized servicemen returning to South Africa. Consequently it was a dry ship – much to Lutyens's annoyance. He wrote to Lady Emily (26 February): 'It is very odd being on a dry ship – and I feel nettled! at the deep pleasure it will give you! bless you. I have drunk nothing but ginger ale – and an occasional lemon squash and tea for tea and tea for breakfast. I have spoken to no woman yet! I have joined up with all the flying boys. They have all killed Huns in the air and they have all crashed – and are full of spirit and adventure.' For most of the time he was busy in the Chart Room revising a set of architectural drawings, only emerging with his stories, doodles and outrageous puns at the Captain's table (figs. 2 and 3).

In Cape Town they stayed with the architect J. M. Solomon – at his house, 'The Woolsack', built by Herbert Baker for Rhodes and Kipling. 'A nice little house', wrote Lutyens (20 March), 'but full of schoolboy error – sort of early me!' And while Ward was entertained by Mrs Solomon, a middle-aged English blonde, Lutyens spent his time at Solomon's office going through his plans for the University. Lutyens had been asked for his views on Cape Town University by

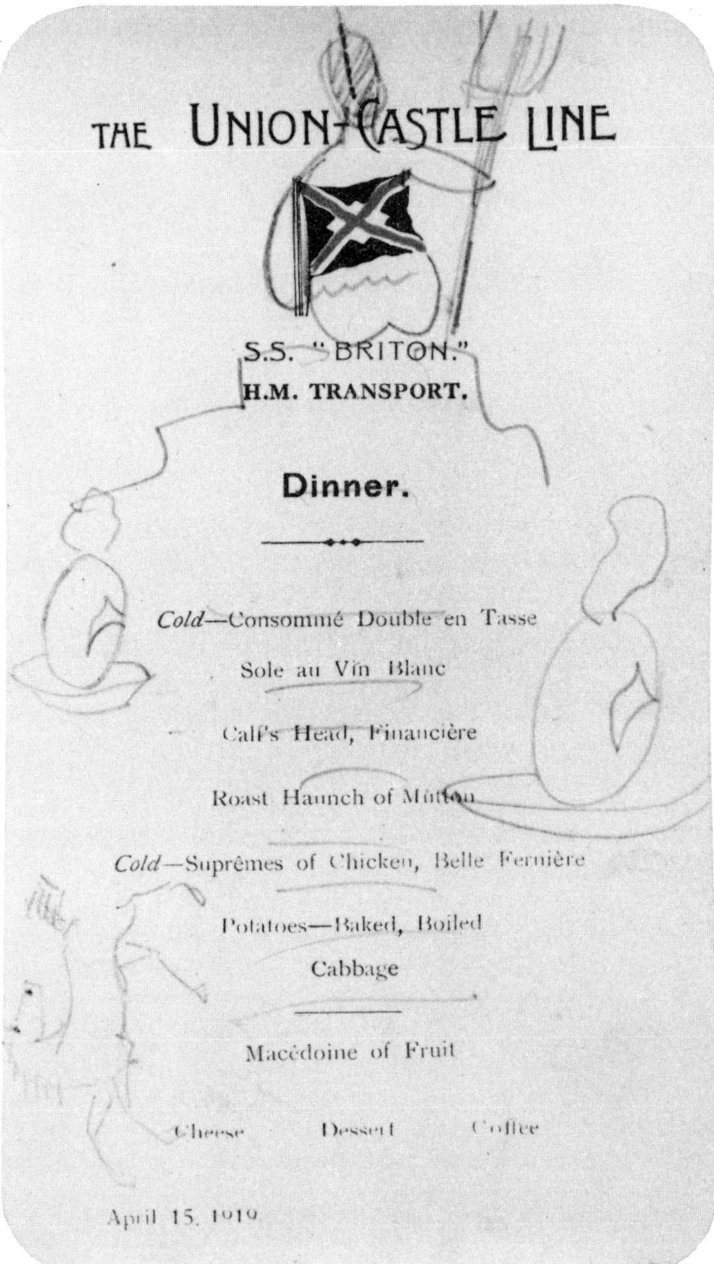
THE UNION-CASTLE LINE

S.S. "BRITON."

H.M. TRANSPORT.

Dinner.

Cold—Consommé Double en Tasse

Sole au Vin Blanc

Calf's Head, Financière

Roast Haunch of Mutton

Cold—Suprêmes of Chicken, Belle Fermière

Potatoes—Baked, Boiled

Cabbage

Macédoine of Fruit

Cheese Dessert Coffee

April 15, 1919

2 Menu, SS *Briton*, 15 April 1919, with Lutyens's doodles. (Herbert Ward)

3 Doodle by Lutyens: two people taking off their shirts in a small cabin. (Herbert Ward)

General Smuts as early as 1910, and had prepared designs, hoping that he and Baker would be asked to build it. But the financial setbacks of war put an end to these hopes, and in 1918 Solomon, a pupil of Baker's, was given the commission and Lutyens was invited to be consultant. Lutyens wrote a good report on Solomon's plans – 'most excellent, and I can suggest no better way for ecomony or effect' – but later the expense proved too great for the South African government, and Solomon shot himself at his home, eighteen months after Lutyens's visit.

But Lutyens was not to know of this tragedy in April 1919 when, with his work complete and nothing much to do, he set sail on the return voyage on the RMS *Briton*. The Master of the *Briton* was Captain Edward Weatherston Day (1860–1930), a small round man with a white beard. He had been at sea all his life, first joining the Union Castle line in the 1890s, and having his first command of a ship in 1906. He had had a gallant naval career in the war, captaining transport and hospital ships, and was awarded the Lloyds Silver Medal twice for saving lives at sea. In 1917 Day was Captain of the *Glenart Castle*, a hospital ship, which was mined and torpedoed twelve miles off Portsmouth. Day managed to achieve the safe disembarkation of 525 wounded soldiers into lifeboats and successfully brought the sinking ship to Portsmouth. (Later, in 1922, Day also rescued all the passengers from the German liner *Hammonia* which sank off Cape Finisterre.)

Lutyens obviously warmed to the heroic sea-dog (figs. 4 and 5), and enjoyed drinking with him, as he took enormous pleasure in meeting people of character. He had little to do on the voyage. The weather was calm. He was not a reader (although he did enjoy Hazlitt's *Table Talk*), but loved playing patience and chess. He and

4 Lutyens with Captain Day on the S S *Briton*, 1919. (Herbert Ward)

5 Lutyens on the SS *Briton*, wearing the Captain's cap. (Herbert Ward)

Ward became friendly with Perceval Landon, the *Times* correspondent, who had been on Younghusband's expedition to Tibet in 1904, and Lutyens often played chess with him. When Captain Day said that he wanted to build himself a house at Gravesend when he retired, which he was to do shortly, Lutyens was delighted and set to, commandeering the Chart Room for doing his drawing.

Ward recalls that the house was a 'perfect square on squared paper'. The elevation was of five bays as shown in the model on page 14, and inside, centrally placed, was a square staircase well the full height of the house. The ceiling above the staircase was coved, with in the centre 'a great allegorical painting representing nothing less than the Apotheosis of the Captain'. A gallery ran around the well at first floor level with a balustrade of life-belts. The wall facing the top of the stairs was covered with a map of the world marked with all Captain Day's travels. The house was to face onto the river at Gravesend, and along the retaining wall there were to be miniature ship's life-boats, slung on davits and filled with scarlet geraniums.

Unfortunately, the actual design drawings for the house itself have been lost, and these sheets showing the inventory of its contents are all we have left – obviously taken by Lutyens back to London and then posted to Captain Day in Southampton.

(Captain Day's Mate also wanted a house. This was to be built at Cuffley, where a Zeppelin had been brought down in flames a few years before, the first enemy aircraft to crash on British soil. Lutyens handed this job to 'Wardie', who took the commission very seriously, working away in the cabin he shared with Lutyens. He produced a splendid symmetrical house with sloping overhung roof and a matching pair of triple-arched loggias on the garden front. He ran into difficulties with the roof and flues but Lutyens pointed out the mistakes and encouraged him, saying that it was the Devil who gave men pencils and God who gave them india rubbers.)

Captain Day never built his house. He had only a captain's pay and possibly the design was a little grand. He lived all his life in rented accommodation in Southampton. Neither did the Mate build. 'He probably came to the conclusion,' said Lutyens to Ward, 'that your loggias would make Cuffley forget its Zeppelin.'

Back in England, Ward went in September to read architecture at London University, and Lutyens turned to the Cenotaph.

Surprisingly few sets of imaginary drawings of the nature of Captain Day's house survive, although Lutyens must have produced many similar ones to delight or win over prospective clients.

So often clients were friends or became friends long before the house was built.

There are two surviving sketchbooks, datable to 1891–5, that are very comparable in spirit with Captain Day's house. The first is a small sketchbook made for C. D. Heatley, containing designs for Munstead Corner. The second, made for Gertrude Jekyll, contains an early design for Munstead Wood, made in about 1893. This little book, in watercolour and pen throughout, has the same projection into an imaginary world. Not only are there exterior views of the house from every angle, but also vignettes of stairs and landings, corridor doors with brooms and steaming coffee pots, oaken chests, logs under the stairs and laden Surrey sideboards (fig. 6).

Christopher Hussey in his biography of Lutyens makes the apt comment, in describing the highly detailed series of letters Lutyens wrote to his wife in 1897–8 discussing their future home: 'It is, perhaps, most significant as a detailed example of the way he projected his imagination into the life to be led in his designs, a life more intense than might ever in fact be led in them.' In 1922, this ability of Lutyens to project into idealised worlds took actual expression in Queen Mary's Dolls' House.

The idea occurred at a dinner party given in 1920 by Sir Herbert Morgan at which Princess Marie-Louise, Lutyens and, it seems, E. V. Lucas were present. It was to capture, at a scale of one inch to one foot, a house of the 1920s exact in every detail. This, as well as being a prime example of British craftsmanship at the Wembley Exhibition of 1924, would be a token of respect and affection for the Queen. A great many people, artists and craftsmen, contributed towards the Dolls' House, and a list of these is contained in *The Book of the Queen's Dolls' House*, edited by A. C. Benson and Sir Lawrence Weaver and published in 1924. But someone had to act as coordinator and that someone was Lutyens, who presided over the enterprise with both efficiency and a keen sense of fun. He designed the house, much of its furniture, and was its 'architect' in the same way as he coordinated and designed the Viceroy's House in Delhi. The Delhi office at Apple Tree Yard, and later Mansfield Street, served as a workshop for the Dolls' House. A letter of 17 August shows Lutyens's involvement: 'I have had the first estimates for dolls' house furniture – thirteen state portrait frames £50. The house itself goes on. The Queen writes she is nervous as to how the Doll's house opens. She wants to be able to open it herself without the help of servants – so she can play with it without calling servants! Can't you see the Queen going hush hush to play with dolls!'

There are also in the RIBA surviving sheets of doodles for the

6 Proposed sideboard for the dining room, Munstead Wood, Surrey, for Gertrude Jekyll, 1893. (Munstead Wood Sketchbook, RIBA (Jane Ridley))

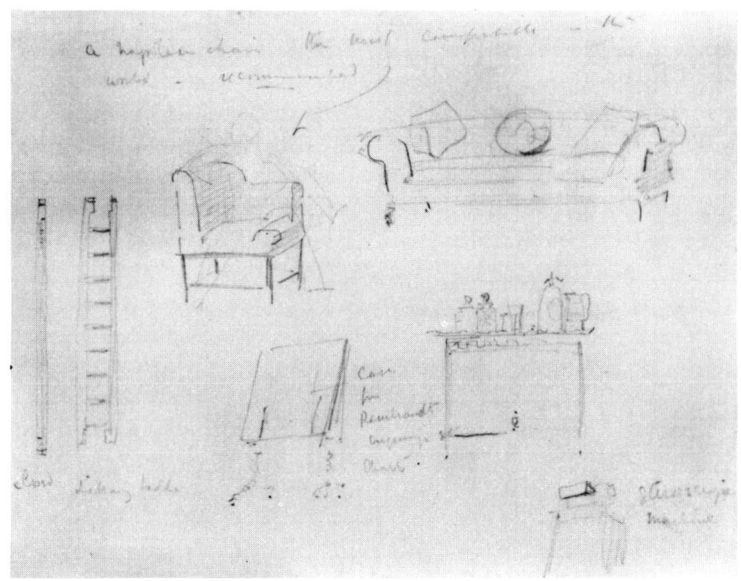

7 Sketches for library furniture for the Queen's Dolls' House, *c*. 1921. (RIBA, Lutyens [242.8])

contents of the interior, very similar in spirit to Captain Day's house but not so highly finished. One sheet shows the library, again with a Napoleon chair, labelled 'the most comfortable in the world – recommended', a library ladder that closes onto a pole (later realised at Blagdon), a wood box, coal scuttle, leopard rug and a case for Rembrandt engravings and charts (fig. 7).

Lutyens's architecture is able to appeal on different levels. There is the linear massing and complex geometry of his forms: the pretence of his building in seeming two to three hundred years old, and the intricacy and surprises of his planning. And there are the details. Some of these are intellectual, in the Mannerist tradition, like the disappearing pilasters on the Midland Bank, Poultry; and others, like oak pegging, blank dormers and consciously expressed drain-pipes, belong to the Vernacular. But some, like his doodles, are created just for fun, and are treats to be collected, like the wheel-barrow garden seat, napkin holders on tapering pilasters, chandeliers made of chickens with broken eggs exploding into light, clocks in the shape of flunkies and clock keys in the form of pansies.

This is the side of Lutyens that created the drawings for Captain Day's House – a spirit best summed up in the dedication to Queen Mary for her Dolls' House: 'Presented to the Queen by Sir Herbert Morgan and some others who wish to promote the greater by the less.'

INVENTRY
& SOME
INVENTIONS

INVENTRY &
SOME INVENTIONS

LIVING ROOM

Blue brown and white
Great sofa & no farther sort
2 arms

The Napoleon chair was Lutyens's favourite design for an armchair. He labels it 'the most comfortable in the world – recommended' in his sketch for furniture for the Queen's Dolls' House Library, c. *1921, and he had two in his own drawing room at Mansfield Street, 1921. He also used the design again at 120 Pall Mall, 1931.*

Work table for Mrs Captain
Table
Pewter ink pot

A design much used by Lutyens, made of oak with plain feet and stretchers, based on seventeenth-century farmhouse furniture which Gertrude Jekyll so admired. Similar examples can be seen at Lindisfarne Castle and Campion Hall, Oxford.

Piano lashed to wall
Copper coal scuttle
glove for coals

INVENTRY & SOME INVENTIONS

LIVING ROOM.

Blue brown & white

Great sofa – & no further sort

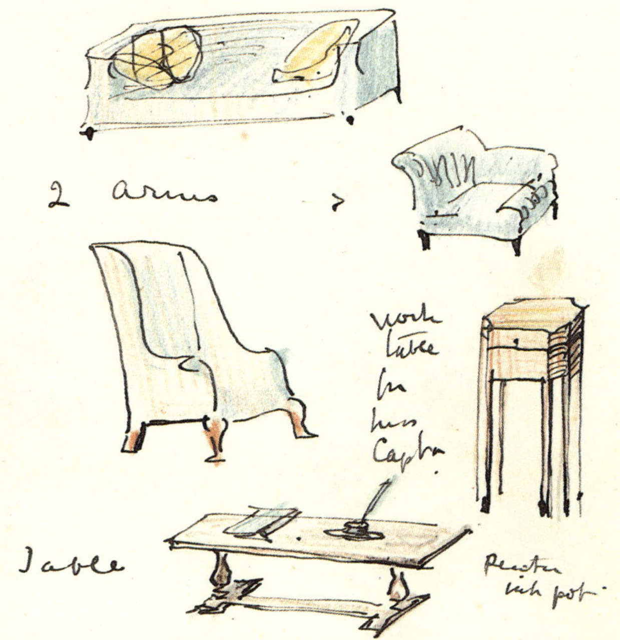

Piano lashed to wall

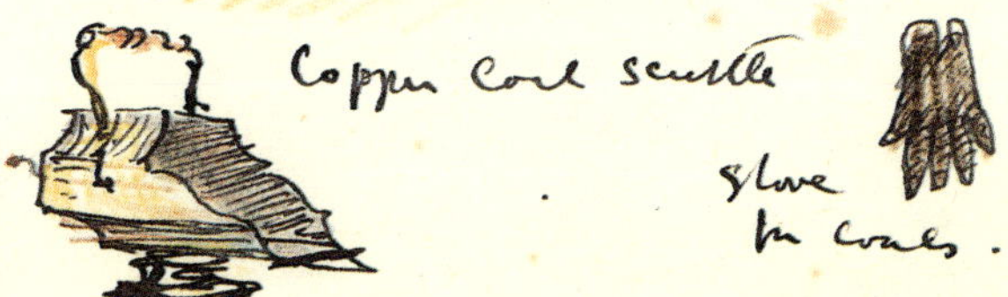

LIVING ROOM

FLOOR to be of narrow deal boards caulked.
brown horse hair carpet with white line
Blue linen curtains
white roller blinds
grand-father clock

window seat

Colored prints of Shipping & Ports
Robinson Crusoe & Friday

and a black cat

Captain Day had no cat – but often took his dog on voyages

ship's Bucket for waste paper basket.
Roll Top Writing Table for Mrs Day
stool

LIVING ROOM

FLOOR to be of narrow deal boards caulked.

brown horse hair carpet with white line

Blue linen curtains white roller blinds

Grand-father Clock

Colored prints of Shipping & Ports.

Robinson Crusoe & Friday

window seat.

and a black cat

Ship's Bucket for waste paper basket?

Roll Top writing Table for Mrs Day

stool

LIVING ROOM

Fireplace.
The cat, the Parrot & dogs

Captain Day's son, R. W. Day, remembers that his father often returned home from sea with a parrot.

the chest for wood.
the kettle crane
the pipe & tobacco
shovel & tongs
no poker not for wood!
The glove and daguerotypes –
The costumes complete of Nubian lady [?]
& other objects of virtue

This inglenook fireplace is very reminiscent of the 'Old West Surrey' vernacular fireplace Lutyens designed for Gertrude Jekyll at the Hut, Munstead. Other examples are the dining room fireplace at Little Thakeham, and the drawing room fireplace at Barton St Mary, Sussex. The archaeology of Old West Surrey life – the fire-dogs, kettle crane, chimney curtain and fire-irons – is well presented.

LIVING ROOM.

Fireplace..

The cat. the Parrot & dogs.
the chest for wood.
the kettle crane the pipe
& tobacco. Shovel &
tongs. no poker not for
wood! the glove.
daguerrotypes. The costumes
complete to Nubian lady
& other objects of virtue.

THE COMPANION HALL

books books books.
a Romford grate
The weather vane clock
& an anoeroid barometer & mirror
to see your bonnet is straight.
Chairs and tables to taste
along wall opposite.
The mat in the lobby
& sofa to lie on after
exercising the mud off the boots

The boots

The style of the hall changes from the vernacular of the living room to modest Georgian, almost exactly similar in style and scale to the Big Room in The Dormy House, Walton Heath, Surrey. The weather vane clock was often used: for example at Lindisfarne Castle, Whalton Manor and Nashdom.

THE COMPANION HALL

BOOKS

Books books books — a

Romford grate

The weather vane clock

& an aneroid barometer

& mirror to see your

bonnet is straight.

Chairs & tables to taste

along wall opposite.

The mat in the lobby

& sofa to lie on after

exercising the mud off

the boots

The boots

THE COMPANION HALL

Looking south over the
garden to the sea see?
on either side of the Porch
is a bay one for Mrs
& the other for Capt. Day
Happy days!

The 'electrolier' was Lutyens's 'ideal' pattern and used at his own home, 29 Bloomsbury Square, and many other places.

THE COMPANION HALL

Looking south over the garden & the sea see?

On either side of the Porch is a bay one for Mrs & the other for Capt. Day

Happy days!

DINING SALOON

6 painted arm chairs in blue
4 silver candlestick with red shades
a portrait of the Captain Day on board the R.M.S. Briton
a book case for books of reference
a side board with a wine cooler

'Wheelback' dining room chairs: this particular design was first used at the Country Life *offices in 1904 and later at 120 Pall Mall, 1931, and at Campion Hall, 1935–7. The wall clock was used at many houses.*

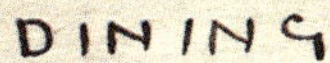

DINING SALOON No 6

6 painted arm chairs · in blue

4 silver candlestick with red shades.

a portrait of the Captain Day on board the R.M.S. Briton

a book case for books of reference

a side board with a wine cooler

DINING SALOON

on the wall a ship in a glass bottle
The kettle holder & kettle
& fireirons & fender

DINING SALOON No. 7.
on the wall a ship in
a glass bottle
the kettle holder a kettle
a fireirons + fender

ACCOUTREMENTS

More especially pertaining to Mrs Day
& these to the Captain
Brandy & Van de Hum
claret champagne sherry Port starboard
salt mustard pot
pepper knife fork spoon spoon egg! laid to *day*
bone spoon for eggs
Captains Cutlass for bread & wedding cakes

ACCOUTREMENTS
8.
more especially pertaining to hers Day
& these to the Captain
Brandy
& Van der Hum
claret
champagne
sherry
port
starboard
salt
mustard pot
pepper
knife
fork
spoon
spoon
Egg! laid to day
bone spoon for Eggs.
Captain's Cutlass for bread & wedding cakes.

VAN DE HUM CUPBOARD & WINE CELLAR

Dry day
Hum day
Rum day
Hock day
Port day with a wife in it!
Sherry day some times "good"
Burgun day
Champ any day

This was a seven-day weekly drinking calendar made by Lutyens for Captain Day. Van de Hum was a South African liqueur. Lutyens often called someone a Van de Humbug.

VAN DE HUM
CUPBOARD
A WINE CELLAR.
9
Dry day.
Hum day
Rum day
Hock day
Port day
Sherry day
sometimes
"good"
Burgun day

OFFICES

from gallery to gal
Beer kitchen clock Roller Towell Coffee mill
Pan bread mouse trap sieve nut meg grater
saucepan Frying Pan whisk salt coffee pot
moulds dish cover
absorbed in Tit Bits

OFFICES
Beer
XXX
kitchen clock
Roller Towel
Coffee mill
Pan
bread
mouse
trap
nut meg grater
sieve
Saucepan
frying Pan
coffee pot
SAL
whisk
Salt
moulds
dish covers
absorbed in Tit Bits

THE STAIRCASE

On the main wall a map of the world
with the Captain's travels marked.
The 'Briton' please note goes anywhere!
on the ceiling a great allegorical painting
representing nothing less than the Apotheosis of
the Captain DAY.

*This square staircase-well rose centrally, the full height of
the house. Life-belts formed the balustrade, a ship's lantern the lamp.
The figures on the painted ceiling toss life-belts.*

THE STAIRCASE
11
On the main hall
a map of the world
with the Captain's travels
marked. The "Briton"
goes anywhere!
On the ceiling a great
allegorical painting
representing nothing less than
the Apotheosis of the Captain
DAY

as to the door on the right we will not enquire.
the other is to the Bath Room.
If you do not knock you may be surprised
& find the Captain in his bath.
Note he rises with the sun a new day.

Note the sun's rays through the window.

CONCERNING
BATHROOMS 12
as to the door
on the right
we will not
enquire.
the other is to
the Bath
Room.
If you do
not knock you
may be surprised
BATH MAT
& find the Captain
in his bath.
Note he rises
with the sun a new
day.

IN THE BED ROOM

we say good night to day
The white sheeps skin mat where on he softly trod
catches the light from the embers of his fire.

IN THE BEDROOM

we say good night
to day

The white Chesha skin mat
where on he softly trod
catches the light from
the embers of his fire

& yet another
Day!

The doll's house is a model of Captain Day's house.

& yet another
Day!